SCREAMING EAGLES

SCREAMING EAGLES

IN ACTION WITH THE
101st AIRBORNE DIVISION (AIR ASSAULT)

PATRICK H. F. ALLEN

Foreword
W. C. WESTMORELAND
General, United States Army, Retired

MALLARD
PRESS

MALLARD
PRESS

An Imprint of BDD Promotional Book Company, Inc.
666 Fifth Avenue, New York, N.Y. 10103

"Mallard Press and its accompanying design
and logo are trademarks of
BDD Promotional Book Company, Inc."

Copyright © 1990 The Hamlyn Publishing Group

ISBN 0792-45323-9

First published in Great Britain in 1990
by The Hamlyn Publishing Group Limited,
a division of The Octopus Publishing Group,
Michelin House, 81 Fulham Road, London SW3 6RB

Produced by Mandarin Offset.
Printed and bound in Hong Kong.

CONTENTS

FOREWORD

The 101st Airborne Division traces its lineage to the 101st Division, formed on July 23, 1918 as part of the mobilization for World War I. Originally the 101st Airborne Division was made up of one parachute regiment, two glider regiments and three artillery battalions.

The 'Eagle Patch' was adopted on May 23, 1923 and represented 'Old Abe' the famous eagle mascot of the 8th Wisconsin Infantry Regiment during the Civil War. 'Old Abe' actually went into battle with the regiment (he was wounded twice), screaming his fury at the enemy while tethered to a wooden shield. His sheer tenacity and fighting spirit lives on to this day, and the 101st Airborne Division is well known throughout the world as the 'Screaming Eagles'.

When Brigadier General William C. Lee assumed command of the 101st Airborne Division on October 19, 1942, he declared to his new recruits: 'The 101st Airborne Division . . . has no history, but it has a rendezvous with destiny'. This declaration is legendary, and, over the years has inspired thousands of men and women to attain the highest mental and physical standards. Throughout the fall and winter of 1942, Lee helped to establish a whole new tactic of warfare—the use of airborne troops in battle.

On October 4, 1974, the 101st Airborne Division (Air Assault) became the first air-assault division in the United States Army and the first in the world. One of the first tasks for this elite force was to establish an Air Assault School and set the required training standards to develop the combined arms concept of air-assault. This is not just the movement of troops from one location to another but a combined arms team, which is highly mobile on land or in the air, and is supported at all times by air reconnaissance and attack helicopters. The 'habitual association' policy ensures that aviation units work regularly with the same ground units, thereby increasing the overall effectiveness of the whole team. Air-assault has become one of the most formidable and important assets on the modern battlefield.

Having exchanged their parachutes for helicopters, the Screaming Eagles continue their proud airborne tradition and today they are at the forefront of Army Aviation and Air Assault concepts. As a powerful and versatile division, the 101st Airborne is ready as part of the Rapid Deployment Force, to meet any challenge, however tough, however demanding.

W.C. WESTMORELAND
General, United States Army, Retired

PART
1

THE
101st
AIRBORNE
TODAY

SCREAMING
EAGLE COUNTRY

HOME OF THE BEST
AND MOST POWERFUL DIVISION
IN THE WORLD

"SALUTE WITH PRIDE"

Far left
**Major General
William C.
Westmoreland's
famous UH-1A
Huey stands in
front of the
division's
headquarters
building. Built in
1959, this was one
of the earliest
Hueys; it was
assigned to the
101st Aviation
Battalion and used
as a command
helicopter by
General
Westmoreland.
After 12 years'
active service it
was retired on
February 13th,
1975.**

FORT CAMPBELL

Fort Campbell, Kentucky, became the home of the 101st Airborne Division on April 1, 1956 and remains so to this day. It is located in the heartland of the United States, astride the Tennessee/Kentucky border and some 65 miles northwest of Nashville, Tennessee. The fort is named in honor of Brigadier General William Bowen Campbell, the last Whig Governor of Tennessee. He was elected Colonel of the First Tennessee Volunteers, the 'Bloody First', and is remembered in popular history for his cry of 'Boys, follow me!' as he led his regiment in the storming of Monterey in 1846.

The site was selected on July 16, 1941, with construction beginning February 4, 1942. Within a year the reservation designated Camp Campbell was developed to accommodate one armored division and various support troops or a total of 23,000 men.

Camp Campbell became the home of the 12th, 14th and 20th Armored Divisions, Headquarters IV Corps and the 26th Infantry Division. In 1969, the 11th Airborne Division arrived and remained until March, 1949. During April 1950 the post became a permanent installation and was redesignated Fort Campbell.

On September 21, 1956 Secretary of the Army, Wilbur M. Brucker and Army Chief of Staff General Maxwell D. Taylor, presented the colors of the 101st Airborne Division to Major General T.L. Sherburne, the first commander of the new ROTAD airborne division. This was the official ceremony which reactivated the 101st Airborne Division after their disbandment at the end of World War II.

In July 1965 the 101st Airborne Division's First Brigade left for duty in Vietnam, followed by the remainder of the division in December 1967. During this period two new units activated at Fort Campbell: a U.S. Army

Left
Fort Campbell, Kentucky, has been home to the 101st since April 1, 1956.

training center in March 1966 and the 6th Infantry Division on November 1, 1967. The Training Center continued to be active on post for more than five years.

Fort Campbell welcomed the 173rd Airborne Brigade in September 1971 and on January 14, 1972 the 'Sky Soldiers' inactivated, most of their personnel and equipment transferring to the 101st Airborne Division (Airmobile). Over the next four months, units of the 101st Airborne Division returned from Vietnam and on April 15, 1972 the Army Training Center closed.

Over the years Fort Campbell has continued to expand to ensure that soldiers of the air-assault division, as well as those of the many other active duty, National Guard and Army reserve units, have the very finest training facilities and living conditions. The post has over 4,100 family housing units, numerous schools, health-care centers (including a modern hospital), shops and sporting facilities.

The training reservation adjacent to the post covers an area of more than 105,000 acres. This includes six large parachute-drop zones, numerous tactical airstrips, and a full array of small-arms, anti-armor and artillery ranges. It also includes a new, versatile multipurpose range complex, and tens of thousands of acres of maneuver area which permits fully integrated, combined-arms training exercises to take place.

Fort Campbell has two airfields, Campbell Army Airfield and Sabre Army Airfield. Campbell AAF provides the division's large helicopter fleet with maintenance and operational facilities and is one of the largest and busiest military airfields in the United States. The 12,000-foot active runway, vast ramp space and rapid-refuelling facilities easily accommodate the largest USAF transport aircraft, ensuring that the air-assault division can achieve rapid-deployment contingency missions anywhere in the world in 18 hours.

Sabre Army Airfield is used primarily for helicopter activities and is home to the Apache helicopters of 1st Battalion, 101st Aviation Regiment and the helicopters of the 2nd Squadron, 17th Cavalry Regiment. The remainder of the Aviation Brigade's helicopters are located at Campbell AAF.

5th Special Forces Group (Airborne) and Task Force 160

Fort Campbell is also home to the 5th Special Forces Group (Airborne) who arrived on June 10, 1988 from their former home at Fort Bragg, North Carolina. Another unit resident at Fort Campbell is that of Task Force 160 'Night Stalkers'. Formed in 1980 from elements of the 101st Aviation Group, it became the 160th Aviation Battalion in 1981 and the 160th Special Operations Aviation Group in 1986. Known today as the 160th Special Operations Aviation Regiment, its modified UH-60s, AH-6s, MH-6s and MH-47Ds use the excellent facilities at Campbell Army Airfield.

AIR ASSAULT

The 101st Airborne Division (Air Assault) is the only air-assault division in the world. The division integrates organic helicopter and ground forces into a combined arms team capable of deploying and manœuvring armor-defeating forces over much larger battle areas than ever before.

During the Vietnam War intensive use of helicopters for both tactical maneuver and combat supply became the norm. The general terrain and tactics used enforced great reliance on helicopter-borne troops. The first division to become totally helicopter-borne was the 1st Air Cavalry Division; it was followed by the 101st Airborne Division, who became the 101st Air Cavalry Division as they acquired their own helicopter aviation group. Later this would be expanded into the airmobile concept.

These infantry would be flown to designated landing zones by their troop-carrying UH-1 Huey helicopters, where they would deplane. Armed reconnaissance helicopters would be used to escort these 'slicks', taking out enemy anti-aircraft guns and protecting landing zones with rockets and gunfire. Larger helicopters, such as the CH-47 Chinook, would provide re-supply or lift artillery units and materials to the many fire-support bases used throughout Vietnam. These bases were essential for providing artillery cover to infantry patrolling the jungles.

The mobility and versatility gained by these air-transported infantry units provided the basis for future air-assault operations. The air-assault concept should, however, not be confused with these earlier heliborne operations. Air assault is a combined-arms concept that is divisional in strength, with its own infantry, anti-tank, support and aviation brigades. This provides a self-contained, highly mobile and flexible unit, capable of

Left
The UH-60 Black Hawk is the workhorse of the Air Assault Division. Powerful, survivable, and highly versatile, it has added significantly to the division's warfighting capability.

Previous pages
'Honor Eagle' ceremonies are held to welcome or to bid farewell to the top three division Generals or the senior Colonel, or to mark national holidays. Ceremonies begin with the presentation of colors.
Inset **During an 'Honor Eagle' to bid farewell to the Assistant Division Commander, an engraved 105mm shell case is presented by a soldier from the Division Artillery.**

Right, top and bottom AH-1S/F modernized Cobras and the AH-64 Apache – the latest and most powerful helicopter in the Army's inventory – give the Air Assault Division unprecedented firepower and flexibility. Both helicopters are equipped to fly at night and can provide responsive and decisive firepower from great stand-off ranges.

movement by air and able to fight on the ground as a combined arms team supported by air reconnaissance and attack helicopters.

Integrated training and combined-arms execution in battle include the movement of air-assault elements close to the objective, while air cavalry and attack helicopters provide reconnaissance and anti-tank capabilities on call to ground units. These tactics are different from the airmobile concept, which essentially deals with transporting forces by air from one location to another.

The air-assault division is tactically flexible, providing a versatile and powerful resource capable of exploiting rapidly changing tactical conditions. It is able to move around the battle area without regard to terrain, reinforcing key positions or conducting deep-strike missions behind the forward edge of battle area (FEBA) or of conducting cross-FLOT (forward line of own troops) operations.

Division Capabilities
The key element of the air-assault division is its three infantry brigades. Each has a brigade headquarters plus three air-assault infantry battalions.

Supporting the infantry brigades is an aviation brigade. This has three assault helicopter (UH-60A Black Hawk) battalions, one medium helicopter (CH-47D Chinook) battalion, two attack helicopter battalions (AH-1S/F Cobras and AH-64A Apaches), an air cavalry squadron and a command and control/utility battalion. The division artillery (DIVARTY) comprises a headquarters battalion with three 105mm howitzer battalions, plus a 155mm howitzer battalion assigned in general support to the division.

The division support command is composed of a maintenance, supply and transport battalion, an aviation maintenance battalion, and a medical battalion. This last includes an air ambulance company equipped with UH-60 Black Hawk MEDEVAC helicopters.

Air-Assault Infantry Brigades
The fighting heart of the division is its three air-assault infantry brigades. The primary mission of all other units in the division is to provide the combat support and combat-service support necessary to assure the success of the brigades in battle. Each year the Air Assault School graduates thousands of 'Screaming Eagles' as well as hundreds of soldiers from other units. The air-assault soldier is the key element in combat and must demonstrate a level of fitness, discipline and tenacity that sets him apart from other soldiers. The Air Assault School program, touted as the 'Ten Toughest Days in the Army', combines a really demanding physical-training program with an academic curriculum that teaches fundamental air-assault skills.

In support of the infantry brigades the division has almost 200 long-range HMMWVs (High Mobility Multipurpose Wheeled Vehicles) with TOW anti-tank missile systems. Each infantry battalion has three companies, plus one TOW HMMWV company. Each infantry platoon also carries two 'Dragon' man-packed, medium anti-tank weapons. Each infantry soldier may also carry an individual light anti-tank weapon. Indirect fire support is provided to the ground commander through his organic 60mm and 81mm mortars.

Division Artillery
The division has three, 105mm direct-support artillery battalions, plus a general support battery of 155mm howitzers; all are helicopter-portable. Integrated with U.S. Air Force tactical air support, U.S. Navy air- and gunfire, reinforcing systems from echelons above division, and battlefield preparation, the air-assault-division makes an extremely formidable foe.

The Aviation Brigade
The division derives its power from the tactical mobility provided by its fleet of some 300 helicopters. Aviation is integrated into all aspects of the combined-arms combat operations. The division offers a high degree of operational and strategic mobility, since all its helicopters and equipment are capable of being airlifted by Air Force transports.

UH-60 Black Hawk
On the battlefield, most of the division's vehicles and equipment can be transported by its 115 UH-60 Black Hawk and 38 UH-1 Iroquois helicopters. The Black Hawk is a

highly versatile and survivable helicopter which has greatly increased the division's fighting capability. It can move troops, equipment, fuel, and ammunition, and it performs medical evacuations. In most environments it can carry 12 combat-equipped troops plus an external load of over 3,000 pounds. It can also carry the 7,500-pound HMMWV, two 500-gallon fuel blivets, the 105mm howitzer with 40 rounds of ammunition or a variety of other combat loads. Its external wing stores (ESSS) can be used to mount various weapons systems.

The Attack Fleet
The attack fleet consists of the AH-1S/F Cobra and the AH-64A Apache. The Apache is a multi-purpose attack helicopter whose primary missions are to eliminate armor and to provide armed escort for air-assault operations. It is uniquely equipped to fight at night and from great stand-off range it can provide accurate and decisive firepower on call from ground commanders.

The division's 18 Apaches each carry up to 16 Hellfire antitank missiles or up to 76 70mm (2.75in) folding-fin aerial rockets. The pilot or co-pilot/gunner can direct 1,200 rounds of suppressive fire from the single barrel 30mm M203 cannon mounted in the nose chin turret. The helicopter's advanced mission equipment and night-vision capability provide the air-assault division with a powerful strike force at any time in all weather. With the integration of new air-to-air missile systems, the Apache will also be able to provide additional air-to-air cover, as helicopters become increasingly adept at air combat and anti-helicopter operations.

The attack fleet's AH-1S/F (modernized) Cobra helicopters combine the firepower of 20mm cannon, 70mm (2.75in) folding-fin aerial rockets and TOW anti-tank missiles. They can move rapidly to any threatened area and destroy hard targets, such as armored vehicles, bunkers and fighting positions; or softer targets, such as personnel, vehicles and command, control and logistical facilities. They can provide fire support to the ground commander when operating out of range of artillery, and other indirect fire-support systems, as well as escorting troop-carrying formations.

... hold

The Reconnaissance/Scout Fleet

Most scout and reconnaissance duties are carried out by a fleet of over 60 OH-58C light observation helicopters. They perform reconnaissance missions, adjust artillery and mortar fire, control air strikes, position attack helicopters and conduct command, control and liaison missions.

Medium-Lift Helicopters

The medium-lift capability is provided by a fleet of 45 CH-47D Chinook helicopters. The Chinook can carry 25,000 pounds of equipment and is used to transport artillery, ammunition, fuel, large equipment and other heavy, palletized loads. The new Chinook 'D' model has greatly increased logistical support for the division, enabling heavy equipment to be carried farther, faster and at a lower altitude than ever before.

To reduce the vulnerability of helicopters to enemy optical and radar-directed air-defense systems, the division has become highly proficient in tactical and night-flying operations. It is equipped and trained for long-range air-assault operations deep into the enemy's rear areas to destroy key installations, facilities and forces. These 'deep-strike' missions are conducted at night by completely blacked-out aircraft flown by aircrews wearing night vision goggles (ANVIS) and, in the AH-64 Apache, crews using forward-looking infrared PNVS/TADS systems.

The division routinely demonstrates an ability to accomplish its combat missions through tough, realistic training, not only at Fort Campbell but throughout the world. Both ground and aviation elements continually exercise together, adopting the 'habitual association' principle which allows aviation units to work regularly with the same ground units.

Training realism is increased by participation in extensive combined-arms live-firing exercises at the National Training Center at Fort Irwin, California, and at the Joint Readiness Training Center at Fort Chaffee, Arkansas. The use of opposing forces, skilled in Soviet tactics, and other training innovations, such as the use of Multiple Integrated Laser Engagement Systems (MILES), create a realistic combat environment for both

ground and aviation units. At the same time, training costs are minimized by extensive use of battlefield simulations, sub-caliber devices, and helicopter and weapons simulators. All this training is designed to enable the air-assault soldier to survive on today's battlefield and to allow the division to commit as few men as possible to an operation, commensurate with accomplishing the mission.

MILITARY UNITS

The 101st Airborne Division (Air Assault) is organized into the following units.

Infantry Brigades

1st Brigade 'Always First'
Headquarters and Headquarters Company (HHC) 1st Brigade
1st Battalion, 327th Infantry Regiment
2nd Battalion, 327th Infantry Regiment
3rd Battalion, 327th Infantry Regiment
2nd Brigade 'Strike Brigade'
HHC, 2nd Brigade
1st Battalion, 502nd Infantry Regiment
2nd Battalion, 502nd Infantry Regiment
3rd Battalion, 502nd Infantry Regiment
3rd Brigade 'War Eagles'
HHC, 3rd Brigade
1st Battalion, 187th Infantry Regiment
2nd Battalion, 187th Infantry Regiment

Left
The CH-47D Chinook helicopter is remarkably versatile. The triple cargo hook system and capacious fuselage allows it to carry more equipment faster, lower and farther than ever before. DIVARTY (Division Artillery) 105mm howitzers can easily be carried internally to provide additional tactical surprise, or they can be slung loaded.

3rd Battalion, 187th Infantry Regiment

Division Artillery

HHB, DIVARTY

1st Battalion, 320th Field Artillery Regiment (105mm)

2nd Battalion, 320th Field Artillery Regiment (105mm)

3rd Battalion, 320th Field Artillery Regiment (105mm)

Battery C, 5th Battalion, 8th Field Artillery Regiment (155mm)

Aviation Brigade

1st Battalion, 101st Aviation Regiment (AH-64)

3rd Battalion, 101st Aviation Regiment (AH-1 and OH-58)

4th Battalion, 101st Aviation Regiment (UH-60)

5th Battalion, 101st Aviation Regiment (UH-60)

6th Battalion, 101st Aviation Regiment (UH-1)

7th Battalion, 101st Aviation Regiment (CH-47D)

9th Battalion, 101st Aviation Regiment (UH-60)

2nd Squadron, 17th Cavalry Regiment (OH-58C, AH-1 and UH-60)

The Aviation Brigade was formed on July 1, 1968 at Camp Eagle, Vietnam as the 160th Aviation Group. In 1969 it was redesignated 101st Aviation Group with the emergence of airmobile battle doctrines. In August 1986 the 101st Aviation Group became the 101st Aviation Brigade, and in October 1987 became regimentally affiliated.

The 101st Aviation Brigade leads the way in Army aviation innovations and was the first to equip with Black Hawk and Chinook (CH-47D) helicopters.

The mission of the Aviation Brigade is to deploy worldwide and plan, coordinate and execute aviation operations as an integrated element of the Combined Arms Team. It must also locate, identify and destroy enemy forces in joint, combined or unilateral operations and provide the means to deliver the men and materials of the 101st Airborne Division (Air Assault) to the battlefield.

Division Support Command

'The Lifeliners'

HHC, Division Support Command

8th Battalion, 101st Aviation (Maintenance)

326th Medical Battalion

426th Supply and Transportation Battalion

801st Maintenance Battalion

101st Personnel Service Company

101st Finance Support Unit

63rd Chemical Company
53rd Quartermaster Detachment

The mission of the 3,100 soldiers of the Division Support Command is to provide all logistical support—ground and air direct support maintenance, medical and administrative—to the division.

Separate Battalions in the 101st

There are several separate battalions which are part of the division which form an integral part of the total fighting force. These units are:
326th Engineer Battalion
501st Signal Battalion
Law-Enforcement Command
311th Military Intelligence Battalion
2nd Battalion, 44th Air Defense Artillery

Campbell Army Airfield is the home of several U.S. Air Force tenant units. They include Detachment 1,436th Military Airlift Wing, 21st Tactical Air Support Squadron, Detachment 5,507th tactical Air Command, USAF.

Corps Support Group

HHC, U.S. Army Garrison
20th Engineer Battalion (Combat)
20th Replacement Detachment
29th Transportation Battalion
86th Evacuation Hospital
561st Supply Service Battalion
61st Medical Detachment (LB)

The Corps Support Group, formally the Eagle Support Brigade, has a combined strength of over 2,900 soldiers. Its work includes, among many other tasks, transportation support, airfield control, and aviation and ground refuelling support.

HIGHLIGHTS OF AIR ASSAULT

As the Army's 'all-purpose' division the 101st spends a great deal of time on exercise at Fort Campbell and elsewhere in the United States and throughout the world. These exercises are at unit, brigade or division level and may involve only the 101st Airborne Division or they may be joint maneuvers with one or more separate units.

The strength of the air-assault division resides in its combination of firepower with strategic and tactical flexibility. The air-assault force is particularly suitable for screening, covering-force and delay operations, for reinforcing and economy-of-force roles, for rear-area security operations, and for offensive operations such as deep-strike missions into the enemy's rear areas.

These operations can be conducted over all types of terrain and in all weather. Bad weather and poor visibility, in fact, help to conceal the air-assault helicopters in flight and reduce the effectiveness of the enemy's surface-to-air missiles and high-performance aircraft.

The air-assault division also provides a flexible, highly mobile reserve, enabling ground commanders to concentrate forces quickly at a critical time and place. Obstacles such as river crossings, refugee and traffic congestion, and towns and villages which plague ground-force commanders, present no problems for heliborne troops.

The division can lift simultaneously into battle combat elements of several of its nine infantry battalions. Helicopter landing zones (LZs), especially those used for deep strikes and for crossing the forward line of own troops (FLOT), can be prepared and secured by using the special skills of the division's Pathfinder Company. This cadre of specialized troops is the division's only unit that remains on parachute-jump status, and it can be helicoptered or parachuted ahead of air-assault missions for reconnaissance and security tasks. The rapid movement of air-assault forces over long distances to landing zones on or near the objective provides fresh combat troops for battle, eliminating arduous and much slower movements by land transport or on foot. Division howitzers can be moved at treetop level by Black Hawk helicopters flying at 120 knots or transported internally in the Chinook helicopters. Indirect fire support can be massed at critical points at extremely short notice. Day or night, the division artillery undertaking helicopter gun-raids can provide an enormous force multiplier at critical times.

Combat power can be built up progressively by aerial reinforcement and resupply, until the division's total combat force can be brought to bear against the enemy. These forces include ground TOW missile systems which ideally can destroy enemy tanks or armored vehicles at ranges of more than 3,000 meters. Meanwhile AH-1 Cobras and AH-64 Apaches provide an aerial engagement platform capable of massing against enemy armor or defeating it over great distances. The division's helicopters are deployed in the field, along with the troops they will support. Forward arming and refuel points (FARPS) for attack helicopters are established close to the battle area, helping to maintain the high level of anti-armor support for the deployed forces. U.S. Air Force transport aircraft operating from forward tactical airheads provide the continuous strategic support needed by the division.

The command and control structure maintains the tactical initiative, and its flexibility and security, by frequently shifting (often at night) the division's assault command posts, which keep well forward in the battle area. The bulk of the tactical operations centers (TOCs) and supporting signal systems of the headquarters are dispersed to distances of 30 kilometers or more, as required by the tactical situation. Command and control is also ensured by the use of helicopters reporting back directly from the battle areas and by the continued integration of satellite communication systems.

The frequent redeployment of helicopters to the constantly shifting positions of the assault units and their artillery support calls for a high level of skill in nap-of-the-earth (low level) and non-illuminated night-flying techniques. All the division's helicopter crews are experienced in these techniques, which are frequently tested and sharpened in the course of simulator training programs. Multiple Integrated Laser Engagement Systems (MILES), fitted to helicopters during exercises, greatly increase the realism of these programs. The pay-off in aviation proficiency is the high degree of coordination and cooperation that exists between the aviation units and support units of the division; the 'habitual-association' training program has also helped towards achieving this.

Owing to the tactical efficiency and extraordinary firepower achieved by the combined-arms approach, the division does not normally provide for a reserve when planning a given operation. As the battle develops, the need for a ground tactical reserve, as such, is

met by extracting the division's least-engaged force and airlifting it, or by directing attack helicopter units to the critical points of action. The air-assault division is normally assigned to a corps, where its mobility permits its use in a variety of missions throughout the corps area.

Above
A UH-60 Black Hawk with a sling-loaded 105mm Howitzer.

'THE TEN TOUGHEST DAYS IN THE ARMY'

Qualification Criteria for 'The Air Assault Badge'

The Air Assault School based at Fort Campbell, Kentucky, USA has earned a worldwide reputation for excellence, graduating thousands of Air Assault Soldiers—male and female—as well as foreign military personnel.

The challenging curriculum covers all aspects of air-assault operations, including combat, rigging techniques and rappelling.

1 The individual must be rated 'Excellent' in conduct and efficiency.

2 He must be MOS qualified (Military Occupation Speciality).

3 He must qualify with his assigned weapon.

4 He must be assigned to and serve in an air-assault unit.

5 He must pass the 'Ranger/Special Forces' physical qualification test (less the 15 meter swim) in each event. One event is waiverable, but he must achieve a minimum overall score of 350 points.

6 He must satisfactorily complete the Air Assault School program of instruction consisting of the following subjects, air-assault concepts and terms: U.S. Army helicopter familiarization and combat air-assault procedures, including troop-ladder procedures; tower and helicopter rappelling procedures; sling-load procedures; aerial medical evacuation procedures.

7 He must maintain a 70 per cent average mark in three examinations, two written and one oral.

Far left
To gain entry to the Air Assault School a soldier must successfully complete a nine-station obstacle course (two stations being mandatory) and a two-mile run. The 'Confidence Climb' is mandatory: it is easy at the start, but the higher you climb the greater is the distance between the rungs.
Left
Soldiers take a short rest while awaiting their turn at the next obstacle. Even early on a summer morning the humidity is high in Kentucky.
Following pages
'The Belly Crawl'. The school's instructors take only the best candidates.
Inset **'The Weaver' is aptly named. It is not mandatory, but if you start you must finish it or the instructor will send you around again.**

Previous pages
It's down hill all the way as two soldiers near the end of their twelve-mile road march. To complete it within the designated time they are obliged to run as well as march.

Right
The Air Assault School has trained thousands of soldiers since it was established in 1974. Next stop for this soldier is Graduation.

Below
Students pay careful attention to the words of their Instructor. It will be their turn next to rappel from the helicopter.

Above
**The Air Assault
School teaches
soldiers specialized
air-assault
techniques, tactics
and basic skills
such as rigging,
climbing troop
ladders, pick-up
and landing-zone
operations, and
rappelling from
helicopters.**

Right
**Two Air Assault
School instructors
add a leaven of
humor to their
demonstration of
rappelling
techniques.**

Far left, left and below
UH-60 Black
Hawks or UH-1H
Hueys are used to
teach helicopter
rappelling
techniques.

Right
Tactical rappelling and STABO (stabilized tactical airborne body operations) require confidence and skill. They are just two of the ways of getting air-assault soldiers into inaccessible locations by day or night. STABO is ideal for dense jungle operations, with the helicopter hovering above the tree canopy.
Far right
'The Air Assault Badge is not given – it is earned'. This soldier has every reason to be proud.

PART

2

THE 101st AIRBORNE *IN ACTION*

Left
'A' Company, 6th Battalion, Black Hawks pull power as they pick up HMMWVs (high-mobility multi-purpose wheeled vehicles) belonging to the 3rd Battalion, 502nd Infantry Regiment. Weighing 7,500 lb each, the HMMWVs represent a challenge to 'Hawk' pilots when they fly them tactically on air-assault combat missions.

Above
Air assault requires continuous and instant-response helicopter support by day and night. To achieve this, the division's helicopters deploy into the field, close to where they are needed.

41

Left
Two technicians
work on the
transmission of a
5th Battalion
Black Hawk,
while its crew
catches up on
sleep after
carrying out
night-time air-
assault raids.

Above
Pilots with the
101st Aviation
Brigade are expert
in night
operations, long-
range air-assault
operations and
tactical nap-of-
the-earth (NOE)
low-level flying.

Below
Covers are placed
across the Hawk's
cockpit to reduce
reflective glace
that might
advertize the
helicopter's
location. In
forward positions
helicopters must
keep continually
on the move.

Previous pages
As part of the
Rapid Deployment
Force the division
is supported by
USAF transport
aircraft. These
aircraft can fly
men, helicopters
and equipment
around the globe
and re-supply the
division as
required.

Left
After landing on a
tactical airstrip a
USAF C-130 from
314 TAW off-
loads personnel
and equipment.
Above
A CUCV
(commercial
utility cargo
vehicle) from 2nd
Brigade is loaded
aboard a USAF C-
130 for
deployment to a
forward airstrip.

Above
The USAF and Army provide specialists to support operations at tactical airfields. These include air traffic control teams and combat control teams from the 18th Aviation Brigade.

Below
Tactical satellite (TACSAT) communications are important to the division. Apart from the Pathfinders, the only soldiers on parachute 'jump' status are those in the Airborne Advance Team of the 501st Signal Battalion. They can be deployed anywhere on the globe and are the first unit to establish communications on the ground. After landing, a compass bearing is used to locate the estimated position of the satellite. Using an aural tone (voice repeater) a word is sent and its echo is timed. When word and echo coincide the TACSAT dish plus high-gain antenna is on line. This allows the commander to talk globally.

Far right
Army and Air Force ground personnel give taxi-ing instructions to a USAF transport plane.

Below
A 105mm
M-101A1 howitzer
with A22 40-
round
ammunition bag is
maneuvered into
its firing position.
Right
The mission of the
Air Assault
Artillery is to
provide close and
continuous fire
support in any
theater of action.

The division
Artillery can
deliver a variety of
4in projectiles:
high explosive
(HE), rocket-
assisted (WRAP
rounds), 'Willy
Peter' (white
phosphorus),
illumination, and
'Killer Junior', to
name a few.

Following pages
A gun team from
the 1st Battalion,
320th Field
Artillery
Regiment, loads
another round.

Above
A gunner takes
meticulous care in
re-setting his
105mm howitzer
after new
coordinates have
been received from
the battery
operations center
(BOC).

Right
'Killer Junior'
projectiles are
fired on a
horizontal
trajectory with
fuses timed to
explode at about
150 yards range.
They are excellent
for perimeter
security.
Below
An artillery
observation post
checks the
position of an
incoming round
before giving the
battery new range
and deviation
coordinates. Both
laser rangefinders
and the naked eye
are used to spot
incoming rounds.

Above
**Back at the 1st
Battalion, 320th
Field Artillery
Regiment Tactical
Operations Center
(TOC), commanders
work out the next
fire mission.**

Below
This Ranger- and Air Assault-qualified infantry motorcycle scout is with the 502nd Infantry Regiment. Equipped with a 250cc Kawasaki motorcycle, he undertakes high-speed and route-reconnaissance missions for his brigade commander.

Left
'Habitual
Association'
enables aviation
units to work
regularly with the
same ground unit
for total aviation
integration,
including
divisional
artillery.

Far left, left and above
The three direct-support artillery battalions are totally air mobile and can be flown by day or night in support of air-assault units. They can undertake fire missions within minutes of unhooking. With their helicopters loitering nearby they can quickly be repositioned or re-supplied with ammunition.

Previous pages
'C' Battery, 1st Battalion, 320th Field Artillery Regiment ('The Top Guns'), work with a UH-60A Black Hawk from 6th Battalion, 101st Aviation Regiment, as they practise gun lifts. This exercise will have to be accomplished in total darkness during a night gun raid.

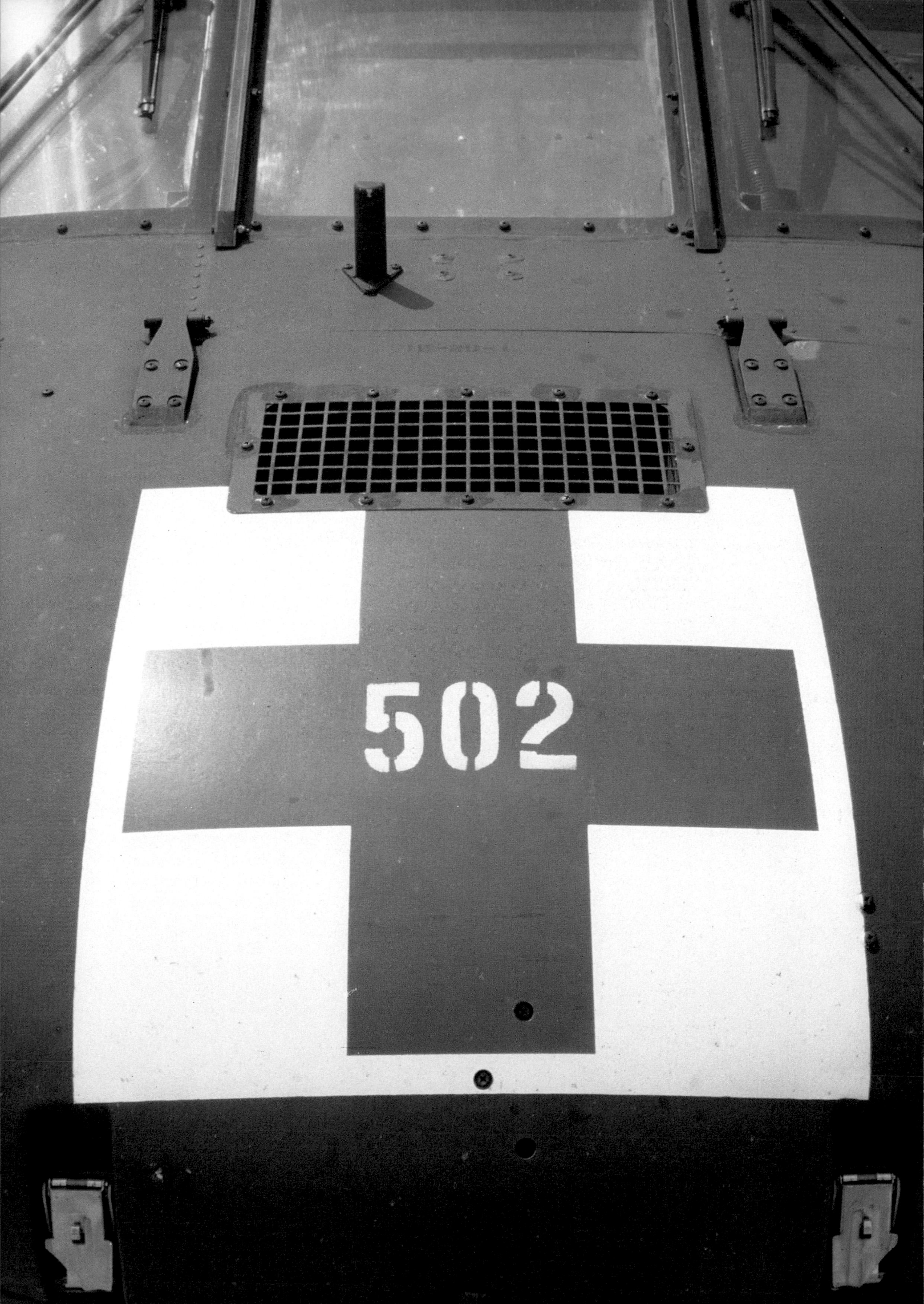
502

Left and right
'D' Company
MEDEVAC Black
Hawks carry four
to six litters plus
comprehensive
emergency
medical
equipment. On
board are two
pilots, a crew
chief, and a flight
medic with
medical
emergency
training. Crews
operating with 'D'
Company, 326th
Medical Battalion,
are among the
most experienced.
In combat they
are required to
operate in hostile
areas undertaking
'dust-off' missions,
picking up injured
soldiers and
aircrews. They
must be well
practised in
tactical flying
techniques and in
the use of night-
vision goggle
(NVG/ANVIS)
equipment, and
must operate in all
weathers.

Previous pages
A MEDEVAC
Black Hawk of 'D'
Company, 326th
Medical Battalion,
hovers as a flight
medic winches up
an injured crew
chief during a
practise 'dust-off'
mission.

Following pages
A HMMWV crew
starts feeling the
weight after
another all-night
operation on day
ten of the war.

Above right
A TOW anti-tank
missile operator
with 'D' Company,
3rd Battalion,
502nd Infantry
Regiment, checks
his sighting
system. The
division has over
200 of these long-
range, vehicle-
mounted systems.

Right
A sentry from
Headquarters
Service Battalion
(HSB), 320th
Field Artillery
Regiment, checks
his weapon while
guarding a
Tactical
Operations Center
(TOC).

Above
A road convoy
from 3rd/502nd
waits for the order
to move out after
it has been
attacked.

Above
Soldiers dig in at
an artillery
observation post.

Left
'B' Company 2nd
Battery, 44th Air
Defense Artillery
Regiment,
provides anti-
aircraft cover. The
Vulcan 20mm
Gatling gun has a
radar-assisted
sighting system
and high-speed
traverse.

Right
This Air Assault
and Ranger
qualified Captain
provides grid
references for a
Gun Battery from
his Forward
Observation Post.

Right
A UH-60A Black Hawk is directed down by a Rappel Master before being rigged for a tactical rappel mission.

Left
**Four STABO
riders walk
towards a Black
Hawk, which rises
slowly as the 90ft
line is taken up.**

Right
A Rappel Master
checks the door as
his 'Hawk' comes
in fast and low
before flaring to a
stop. When the
Rappel Master
signals 'Go!', it's
through the door
and down the rope
in one quick
movement.

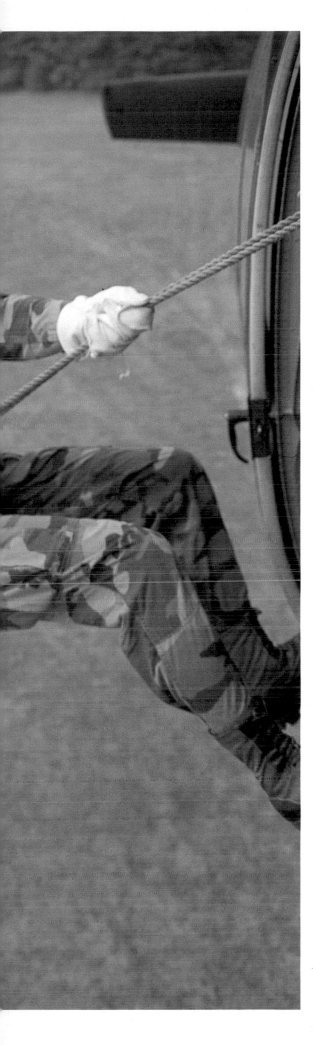

The division's Black Hawks move troops and equipment by day and night. Typical are the night 'gun raids', when Artillery are flown long distances in total darkness to undertake deep-strike missions.

Left
A soldier marshals
in a Black Hawk
at the start of a
mission.
Below
A Black Hawk
crew chief watches
as his helicopter is
refuelled at a
FARP (forward
arming and re-
fuelling point).
Run by the Corps
Support Group,
FARPs are
essential in
maintaining
helicopter
availability to
deployed forces.

Following pages
UH-1H Hueys
from the 9th
Battalion, 101st
Aviation
Regiment, refuel
at a FARP.
Although now
largely replaced by
the Black Hawk,
these modernized
Hueys are still
used in a variety
of roles, including
command and
control.

Left
The crew of a
UH-1H of 9th
Battalion, 101st
Aviation
Regiment, wait in
their Kevlar-
armored seats for
the order to move.
Right
Each Cobra
battalion has
UH-1H Hueys
operating as
command and
control or as DAR
(downed-aircraft
recovery)
helicopters. Armed
with M60 door
guns, plus security
personnel and
technicians, a
DAR team can be
flown quickly to
downed Cobras.
They will secure
the area and then
either repair the
Cobra or recover
the pilot and
gunner and rig the
Cobra for sling
loading by
Chinook.

Right, and below
The AH-1S/F modernized Cobras are operated by 3rd-101st and 2nd Squadron, 17th Cavalry Regiment. Like the other helicopters in the division they can be fitted with MILES (multiple-integrated laser-engagement systems) to create a realistic combat-training environment. As well as simulating the division's own guns, rockets, and missiles, the equipment also registers hits by 'enemy' forces.

Right and below
The Commanding Officer of 3rd Battalion, 101st Aviation Regiment, briefs the crew of an OH-58C Scout helicopter for a mission. The scouts work as a team, finding targets for the Cobras.
Far right
Mortal enemies! An AH-1S Cobra anti-tank helicopter overflies a National Guard tank during exercise 'Mega-Gold'.

Left
The Cobra AH-1S/ F three-barrel 20mm cannon has as 750-round magazine. It can also carry a mix of 70mm (2.75in) folding-fin rockets or eight Hughes TOW missiles. Fitted with a digital fire-control computer, helmet-mounted sights, doppler navigation, secure communications, composite rotor blades, infrared jammer and suppressors, these modernized helicopters are a formidable component of air-assault operations.

Right
A Cobra, using trees as cover, waits for his OH-58C Scout to call him forward for a 'gun-run' along the road.

Above
After being called
up by his OH-58C
'Scout, a Cobra
makes a low-level
dash to his next
firing position.
Using available

cover, he will
unmask only long
enough to engage
the target, before
moving quickly to
another position
to wait for new
targets.

Left
AH-64 Apaches of the 1st Battalion, 101st Aviation Regiment, at Sabre Army Airfield.

Right
The Apache can carry up to 16 laser-seeking Hellfire anti-tank missiles or 76 70mm (2.75in) rocket projectiles (folding-fin aerial rockets).

Following pages
The Apache's 30mm M203 cannon can direct 1200 rounds of armor-piercing suppressive fire by day or night. Primary missions for the division's fleet of Apache helicopters are anti-armor and armed escort for air-assault operations, ideally at night.

Previous pages
The modernized Chinook CH-47D model has the latest night-vision compatible cockpit allowing crews wearing Night vision goggles (ANVIS) to resupply the Division day and night.

Above
The AH-64 is
equipped with a
standard rocket
launcher
containing 19
70mm (2.75in)
rocket projectiles.

Above
Built to survive on
the modern
battlefield, the
Apache AH-64 is
equipped with
'Black Hole' IR
exhaust
suppression, an
ALQ-144 infrared
jammer, chaff
dispensers and a
radar jammer.
Right
An Apache pilot
checks his main
avionics bay prior
to a mission.

Following pages
The Apache's
front cockpit is
occupied by the
co-pilot/Gunner,
with the pilot
sitting behind in
the stepped rear
seat. The two
cockpits are
separated by a
blast-proof
dividing screen
and lightweight
boron armor
shields.

Above and right
The nose of the Apache contains the pilot's night-vision system (PNVS) consisting of a stabilized forward-looking infrared receiver for safe low flying at night. Below this is the target acquisition and designation sight for day and night sighting. This includes a forward-looking infra-red receiver for night operations, a daylight television, and direct-view optics with a laser rangefinder and tracker for daylight operations in poor weather, dust or smoke.

Following pages
An AH-64 Apache from the 1–101 about to lift away from Sabre AAF. Most training is done at night to enable crews to perfect their night-time nap-of-the-earth (NOE) skills. The Apache is supremely well equipped for this type of work.

Left
Both pilot and co-pilot/gunner in the Apache wear the IHADSS (integrated helmet and display sighting system), which projects a thermal image on to a small mirror in front of the right eye. This displays the helicopter's flight information and is also used to cue the main weapon systems (see right) or inform the Hellfire missiles of the target direction.

Following pages
Apache crews from the 1–101st continually train day and night integrating and expanding the helicopter into Air Assault operations. This can be achieved by regular training exercises or using the Apache AH-64 simulator trainer recently installed at Fort Campbell.

Below and right
Three Apache AH-64s from 'B' Company, 1st–101st, move out over the Kentucky countryside to rendezvous with a company of Black Hawks on a deep-strike mission.

Following pages
In the future, Air Assault operations will be carried out almost exclusively at night if they are to be successful. With helicopters like the Apache and with the latest night vision goggles the 101st Airborne Division are in a leading position as they continue to expand the capabilities of modern technology.

Previous pages
Regular live firing of both missiles and guns must be undertaken by the division's Apache and Cobras as they perfect day and night operations.

THE DIVISION 'PATCH'

The patch, insignia and wall-art of the 101st Airborne.

Right, top and below
The 'Screaming Eagle' patch is worn with pride by both men and helicopters of the division. The black painted patch is stencilled on to the nose of a Black Hawk, the only visible sign that this 'Hawk' belongs to the 101st and no other U.S. Army Aviation Battalion.

Page 123
Top Left
The Air Assault coin stems from the Airborne tradition of having a division coin carried by Airborne soldiers depicting the division battle honors together with the owner's name and his graduation number from Airborne training or Air Assault School.
Center left
A large number of Air Assault soldiers wear both Parachute and Air Assault wings on their Battle Dress Uniforms (BDUs).
Bottom left, center right, bottom right
Warrior graffiti has become an art form in its own right.
Top right
The Eagles Conference Room carries the insignia of the 101st Airborne Division.

The 'Screaming Eagle' patch derives from one used by the 8th Wisconsin Infantry Regiment during the Civil War. Depicting the American Bald Eagle 'Old Abe', it was first adopted on May 23, 1923 by the 101st Division. When activated at Camp Claiborne on August 15, 1942 the 101st Airborne Division adopted the eagle patch, but without the flames of the original. On August 29, 1942 the airborne label (tab) was added.

Two changes have been made to the patch since 1942. First, the black shield was worn without the airborne tab when the 101st became a training division in 1948–9 and 1950–3. The second change took place in Vietnam, when the division wore the subdued green and black patch. The original colored patch reverted to a completely black background, behind a white eagle with gold beak and red tongue, after the division returned to Fort Campbell. Today the division uses both the colored and the subdued patch.

In November 1942 the division was given a live eagle mascot, 'Young Abe', presented by the state of Wisconsin. This was a successor to the live mascot 'Old Abe' carried into battle by the 8th Wisconsin Infantry Regiment. (Wounded twice, 'Old Abe', died after the Civil War and his remains were displayed in Wisconsin state capital building until destroyed by fire.) 'Young Abe' trained with the division until his death in 1943. He was replaced by 'Bill Lee I' in 1956—the last eagle mascot to be kept by the division.

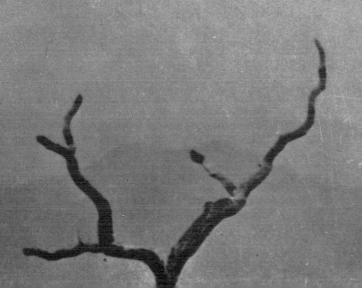

PART
3

THE
101st
AIRBORNE
UNIT HISTORY

During the early part of World War II the use of specially trained airborne troops by Britain and Germany proved highly successful. Before the United States entered the war, in 1941, and following the suggestion of Major William C. Lee, the U.S. War Department on June 25, 1940 formed the first parachute unit, a test platoon. Using aircraft and parachutes borrowed from the U.S. Air Force, the test platoon developed the procedures and methods that would eventually be adopted by the U.S. Army airborne divisions.

The success of the test platoon led to the establishment of several parachute battalions and regiments during the next two years. As with the British and German airborne units, the use of gliders as well as paratroopers was developed, the U.S. airborne divisions eventually forming glider regiments. After this early success, Lee was promoted to colonel, and in the summer of 1942 the commander of the Army ground forces, Lieutenant-General Lesley J. McNair, acted on Colonel Lee's recommendations and ordered the formation of the 82nd and 101st Airborne Divisions.

THE 101st AIRBORNE DIVISION

The 101st Airborne Division traces its lineage to the 101st Division, which was formed on July 23, 1918 as part of the mobilization for World War I. At the end of the war the unit was demobilized, but in 1921 the 101st Infantry Division was formed and reorganized as a reserve unit with headquarters in Milwaukee, Wisconsin. On August 15, 1942 the division disbanded and was reactivated at Camp Claiborne, Louisiana, as the 101st Airborne Division. The initial personnel and equipment for both the 101st and 82nd Airborne Divisions came from the 82nd Motorized Infantry Division, which inactivated at the same time.

Initially the 101st was made up of one parachute regiment (the 502nd Parachute Infantry), two glider regiments (the 327th and the 401st Glider Infantry), and three artillery battalions (the 377th Parachute Field Artillery, the 321st Glider Field Artillery, and the 907th Glider Field Artillery). Additional support units were the 326th Airborne Engineer Battalion, the 101st Signal Battalion, the 326th Airborne Medical Company, and the 426th Airborne Quartermaster Company.

Lee, now promoted to Brigadier General, assumed command of the 101st Airborne Division on October 19, 1942. During his introductory speech to the division, Lee declared to his new recruits: 'The 101st Airborne Division . . . has no history, but it has a rendezvous with destiny'. He also mentioned the eagle emblem, saying, 'Let me call your attention to the fact that our badge is the great American Bald Eagle. This is a fitting emblem for a division that will crush its enemies by falling upon them like a thunderbolt from the skies'.

In October the 101st began rigorous training at Fort Bragg, North Carolina as General Lee helped formulate and establish the new tactics to be used by the division in battle. In June 1943 the 101st received a second parachute regiment, the 506th Parachute Infantry, from Camp Toccoa, Georgia. That summer the division proved itself during the Tennessee Maneuvers and the Army deployed it to England to prepare for the invasion of Europe.

The division sailed to England on September 5, 1943, disembarking 10 days later at Liverpool. Based in Wiltshire and Berkshire, it spent the next 10 months in intensive training. Six days a week units trained on Salisbury Plain, practising their operational roles. Their demanding physical-training program included hikes of 25 miles. In October the division formed its own jump school to train new personnel and key members of non-jump units of the division. By the time of the invasion of France, the school had trained over 400 officers and men.

In January 1944 the 101st, now nicknamed the 'Eagle Division', received a second attached unit, the 501st Parachute Infantry Regiment, which gave the division three parachute infantry regiments. In March the 401st Glider Infantry Regiment detached a battalion to the 82nd Airborne Division. In February of that year General Lee suffered a heart attack and returned to the United States. Major General Maxwell D. Taylor took over command.

From their earliest conception, the Supreme Headquarters, Allied Expedition-

Previous pages
Loaded with combat gear, a member of the 1-501st Infantry Battalion moves out on a reconnaissance operation as a UH-1 Huey brings in additional troops.

Left
**Four members of
the original
parachute test
platoon standing
in the door just
before exiting over
Fort Benning,
Georgia in the
summer of 1940.**
Below left
**A member of the
501st Parachute
Infantry Regiment
descending from
the 250-foot free-
fall tower during
the regiment's
jump training at
Fort Benning.**

ary Forces (SHAEF) had earmarked an important role for the new airborne divisions in the planned invasion of France. The airborne troops would jump in prior to the waterborne invasion forces landing on the beaches. Their job would be to secure the exits from the beachheads and to prevent German reinforcements from reaching those areas. As part of their preparation for the invasion the division participated in army-wide exercises, named 'Beaver', 'Tiger' and 'Eagle', as rehearsals for the opening phase of the landings at Utah Beach (Normandy) in June.

'D'-Day

In May 1944 elements of the division began to assemble at airfields and marshalling areas in the south of England. On June 6, 1944 at 0.15hrs Captain Frank L. Lillyman led his team of 101st Pathfinders out of the door of a C-47 transport plane and landed in occupied France. Behind the Pathfinders came six thousand paratroopers of the 101st Airborne Division in C-47s of IX Troop Carrier Command. Encountering heavy ground fire as

Right
British Prime Minister Winston Churchill and General Dwight D. Eisenhower watch a mass parachute demonstration performed by the 506th Parachute Infantry Regiment, with the 377th Parachute Field Artillery Battalion attached, March 23, 1944.
Below
Landing craft bring the 426th Airborne Quartermaster Company and other supporting elements of the Division into Omaha Beach on the morning of June 8, 1944.

they approached the drop zones, many of the C-47s took evasive action and as a result the paratroopers were scattered over a wide area. By nightfall only 2,500 men had assembled in their units. In an effort to carry out their mission to clear and secure the exits from Utah Beach for the 4th Infantry Division, small groups of soldiers valiantly did the best they could. Major General Taylor could assemble only a little over 100 men, most of them officers, before he set out to secure one

of the causeways leading to Utah Beach. Referring to his brass-heavy group, Taylor remarked: 'Never were so few led by so many'.

An important part of the 101st Airborne Division operations in Normandy was performed by the glidermen. Recognition for the glidermen was slow in coming, but in 1943 they were given their distinctive 'hat patch', and in 1944 they were given glider pay and their own 'wings'.

During the 'D'-Day invasion the gliders were scheduled to make their landing at daybreak on June 6, but, in a last minute change, 'Operation Chicago' became a night landing. Fifty-two gliders formed the first wave, led by the 'Fighting Falcon' glider carrying Brigadier General Don. F. Pratt, assistant division commander. While all the pilots managed to land within two miles of the designated area, only six landed in the zone. Intelligence reports had failed to mention that most of the fields in the area were bordered with hedgerows and four-foot earthen fences topped with trees and bushes. As a result five soldiers were killed in the landings, one of them Brigadier General Pratt.

The second glider action, named 'Operation Keokuk', began at daylight on June 7 and was the first daylight glider operation of the war. This operation, using heavier cargo gliders, delivered 157 personnel, 40 vehicles, 6 guns and 19 tons of equipment to the 101st Division and was crucial to the division's success in carrying out its objectives.

After the seizure of the causeways the 101st proceeded towards their new objective, the capture of the town of Carentan, which lay at the junction point for the two American forces advancing from Utah and Omaha beaches and was a key to the success of the initial phase of the invasion. It took five days of bitter fighting, but the 101st finally pushed the German 6th Parachute Regiment out of Carentan on June 12 and held the town until the arrival of the U.S. armored units from the beachheads. During the attack on Carentan, Lieutenant Colonel Robert G. Cole led the 3rd Battalion, 502nd Infantry in a successful bayonet charge. For this action he became the first member of the 101st to win the Congressional Medal of Honor. The 'Eagle Division' fought without respite for 33 consecutive

Left
C-47 type troop carriers and gliders parked at the Ramsbury Airdrome in Southern England on June 5, 1944 prior to the invasion of Normandy, France.
Below
Paratroopers of the 101st Airborne Division establish and maintain a roadblock somewhere in Normandy, France, on June 9, 1944, while waiting for the back-up of seaborne elements of the invasion force.

Right
First issue of the 101st Airborne Division Association magazine, published in France in 1945. The cover picture features Emerson Rhodes and Taylor Sharp, machinegunners of Company F, 501st Parachute Infantry Regiment.
Below
Members of the 101st Airborne Division receive their last riggers check before boarding a C-47 type troop carrier for the air invasion of Holland.

days; it was a distinguished baptism of fire. As units of the division were relieved, they returned to England to prepare for their next mission. For their action in Normandy, elements of the division received the Distinguished Unit Citation and the division commander was awarded the Distinguished Service Cross.

'Operation Market Garden'

For the rest of that summer the 101st remained in England until selected for 'Operation Market Garden', along with the U.S. 82nd Airborne Division and the British 1st Airborne Division. In this operation, conceived by the commander of the British 21st Army Group, Field Marshal Bernard Montgomery, the three airborne divisions were to jump into a narrow corridor in Holland in order to secure a main highway and its key bridges. This would, it was hoped, enable a British army corps to quickly drive northeastward out of Belgium, cross the Rhine at

Arnhem, and then sweep on towards the Ruhr, Germany's industrial heartland.

On September 17, the 101st jumped into four drop zones between the Dutch towns of Son and Veghel (north of Eindhoven) and set out to seize their objectives. Heavy opposition from elements of several German divisions around the town of Best, a few miles to the west, presented a serious threat to the operation. During this battle, PFC Joe E. Mann of the 1st Battalion, 502nd Parachute Infantry became the second member of the division to win the Congressional Medal of Honor. Two days after the 101st had landed, the first elements of the British Guards Armored Division reached the Americans at Eindhoven, the first Dutch city to be liberated. While the British Airborne Division continued their unsuccessful drive to capture Arnhem, the American paratroopers fought a series of battles as German forces tried to cut the corridor along a 16-mile front. The glider operation associated with 'Market Garden' was among the largest of the war. American troops of the 101st and 82nd Airborne Divisions took off from 17 airfields, the 101st alone using a total of 988 gliders. The sky army was so vast that as planes and gliders were landing over Holland others were still

taking off from their airfields in England. The men and materials brought in by glider once more played a decisive role in the success of a mission. Although the 73-day action was the least publicized of the division's campaigns, the battles of 'Hell's Highway' were the most savagely fought in the division's history.

The Siege of Bastogne

After 'Market Garden' the division deployed to Camp Mourmelon, southeast of Reims in France, to rest and reorganize. On December 18, 1944 the 101st was alerted at Mourmelon-le-Grand to meet the German winter offensive which was thrusting back the Allied front in the Ardennes region of southeast Belgium. The division was given the mission of holding the city of Bastogne which lay at the center of a highway network that covered the eastern half of the Ardennes. The need for rapid movement required that mechanized forces use roads instead of fields in this area.

At 20.30hrs on December 17, the 101st received orders to proceed north to Bastogne and 11,840 Eagle Division soldiers moved out quickly in rain and snow for the 107-mile trip. They traveled in open 10-ton trucks commandeered in Rouen and Paris. Many of the division's soldiers were at that time on leave

Left
A CG-4A is towed off the runway by a C-47 aircraft in England en route for Holland.
Below
Paratroopers of the 101st Airborne Division searching captured German prisoners of war in Eindoven, Holland, on September 18, 1944.

Right
Low-flying C-47s drop desperately needed supplies to the 101st Airborn Division at Bastogne, Belgium.
Below
Brigadier General Anthony C. McAuliffe (center), Lieutenant Colonel Paul Danahy, (left) and Lieutenant Colonel Harry W. O. Kinard, holding one of the road signs marking the village of Bastogne, Belgium on December 28, 1945.

in Paris or the United States, including General Taylor. The acting commander, Brigadier General Anthony C. McAuliffe, led the division to Bastogne. On their arrival the German forces were overunning the lightly protected approaches to the city and McAuliffe directed the 501st Parachute Infantry regiment eastward in the direction of the town of Longvilly, an offensive maneuver that temporarily disorganized the Germans and gave the 101st time to set up defensive positions around Bastogne. Attached to the 101st during this battle was Combat Command 'B' of the 10th Armored Division, the 705th Tank Destroyer Battalion and the 969th Field Artillery Battalion.

On December 20 German troops isolated Bastogne by seizing the last road out of the city. The success of their offensive was now dependent on the defeat of the 101st, and strong German armored and infantry units tried to smash through the American lines, first from the north, then from the south and finally from west of the city: all were beaten back. On December 22 the German commander, Lieutenant Colonel Heinrich von Luttwitz, issued a demand for surrender. General McAuliffe signaled his now-famous reply, 'Nuts!'. Although outnumbered by units from five German divisions, the 101st continued to resist until December 26, when the American 4th Armored Division broke through to Bastogne.

During the siege gliders again proved invaluable. The encircled soldiers of the 101st, dangerously low on ammunition and with over 400 wounded men without medical aid, were re-supplied on the morning of December 26 by cargo gliders, which delivered much needed supplies, litter jeeps, aid men and surgeons.

In the three weeks that followed, the newly nicknamed 'Screaming Eagles' participated in some of the hardest and bloodiest fighting of the Bastogne campaign. Teamed with the

U.S. Third Army, they gradually reduced the German resistance in the area. On January 18, 1945 the VIII Corps relieved the 101st of its task of defending Bastogne. Upon departure, the division received an acknowledgement from the VIII Corps command that read: 'Received from the 101st Airborne Division, the town of Bastogne, Luxembourg Province, Belgium. Condition: Used but serviceable'.

After some light duty in the Alsace region of France, the division returned to Mourmelon-le-Grand, where General Dwight D. Eisenhower presented the division with the Distinguished Unit Citation, the first time that an entire division had received this award.

At the end of March the 101st was deployed to the Ruhr region of Germany without the 501st Parachute Infantry Regiment. The 501st remained in reserve for a proposed (but never launched) raid to free Allied prisoners of war. After the Ruhr, the division moved to southern Bavaria. The last combat mission of World War II for the 'Screaming Eagles' was the capture of Berchtesgaden, Hitler's holiday retreat south of Salzburg. Again teamed with the 3rd Infantry Division, the 101st completed their mission and spent the remainder of the war at Berchtesgaden. Battery 'A' of the 321st Field Artillery fired the last combat round for the division in this operation.

While at Berchtesgaden, the 101st received the surrender of the German XIII SS and LXXXII Corps as well as of a number of prominent Nazis. The 506th Parachute Infantry Regiment captured Field Marshal Albert Kesselring, commander-in-chief of the German forces in the West. The 502nd Parachute Infantry Regiment captured Julius Streicher, editor of *Der Stürmer*, and Obergruppenführer Karl Oberg, the chief of the German SS in occupied France. The division also captured other prominent Germans, including the leading *Blitzkrieg* theorist and armor expert, Colonel General Heinz Guderian; and it was given custody of Hermann Goering's art collection.

The end of World War II marked the beginning of a period of sporadic activity for the 101st. The division inactivated on November 30, 1945 and returned to the

United States. During the next 11 years the 101st activated and then inactivated three times as a training unit; this included periods at Camp Breckinridge, Kentucky, from July 1948 to May 1949 and from August 1950 to December 1953. In May 1954 the division activated at Fort Jackson, South Carolina, remaining there until March 1956, when Fort Campbell, Kentucky, became its new home.

Throughout 1956 Fort Campbell received

Top
Paratroopers of the 101st Airborne Division rummage through the ruins of Hitler's home at Berchtesgaden, Germany, in May 1945.
Center
Members of the 327th Glider Infantry Regiment unloading Hermann Goering's looted art treasures at Unterstein, Germany.
Above left
Major General Westmoreland and General Mancinelli of Italy salute the division and National Colors shortly after the latter's arrival at Campbell Army Airfield, Fort Campbell, Kentucky.

new units and reorganized and trained them under the auspices of Headquarters, 101st Airborne Division (Advance). On September 21, the 101st became the first pentomic division. The uniquely equipped and reorganized division consisted of five self-contained battle groups geared to fight on the nuclear battlefield. During the following nine years, the 101st participated in several important exercises involving the division in nuclear battlefield situations. In September 1957 elements of the 101st went to Little Rock, Arkansas to maintain order during the series of civil rights disturbances. The tact, discipline and courage of the division's troops prevented a possible tragedy.

In early 1964 the 101st ceased to be a pentomic division and underwent major reorganization. The new structure increased the division's firepower and improved its ground mobility, command and control. The division participated in several major joint-service maneuvers, including one in the Mojave Desert. In the spring of 1965, the 'Screaming

Eagles' prepared to send a brigade of infantry and support troops to the Republic of Vietnam.

Vietnam

On July 29, 1965, the 1st Brigade of the 101st landed at Cam Ranh Bay (south of Nha Trang)—the third U.S. Army unit to arrive in Vietnam. From the time they arrived until the time they were joined by the remainder of the division in December 1967, elements of the brigade engaged in continuous fighting, taking part in 26 separate operations. Undertaking numerous airmobile operations, the brigade, in their two and a half years of fighting as a separate unit, traveled 2,500 miles and engaged in operations taking place in three of the four tactical zones of Vietnam.

Called the 'Nomads of Vietnam', the soldiers of 1st Brigade killed 6,000 enemy, captured enough weapons to equip eight enemy battalions, and took 2,000 tons of rice from the Viet Cong. Its medical personnel provided treatment for over 25,000 Vietna-

Right
Infantrymen of the 101st Airborne Division run for their helicopters before a combat assault near Camp Eagle.

mese, and the brigade relocated 15,000 refugees. First Lieutenant James A. Gardner, Specialist 4 Dale E. Wayrynen, and Sergeant First Class Webster Anderson each received the Congressional Medal of Honor.

While the 1st Brigade was engaged in 'Operation Klamath Falls', the 2nd and 3rd Brigades, plus divisional support units, moved from Fort Campbell, Kentucky, to Bien Hoa (north of Saigon) in Operation 'Eagle Thrust'. It was the largest and longest military airlift ever attempted. On December 13, 1967 the Commanding General of the 101st, Major General O.M. Barsanti, reported to General Westmoreland in ceremonies at Bien Hoa that the 101st Airborne Division was ready for combat in Vietnam. In mid-January 1968 the 1st Brigade began operations as part of the full division.

The division's area of operations in Viet-

Above
101st Airborne Division paratroopers cross a stream in Northern I Corps.

135

nam included all of Thua Thien province, with the ancient city of Hue, in the coastal plains, and the A Shau valley in the mountain region to the west.

On January 31, 1968 the North Vietnamese Army (NVA) launched the largest single attack of the war: the Tet Offensive. Throughout the assault the 101st engaged in combat operations, from Saigon in the south to Quang Tri in the north. One platoon from the 2nd brigade battled on the rooftop of the U.S. Embassy in Saigon which was being attacked by Viet Cong commandos. During the Tet Offensive and the follow-up operation, named 'Uniontown', the 101st killed 851 enemy.

Soon after this action, the first extended operation involving the division began. Named 'Nevada Eagle', it lasted 288 days, from May 17, 1968 to February 28, 1969. 'Nevada Eagle' was designed to limit enemy movement through active patrolling and ambushes, to capture or destroy the enemy's rice-gathering forces, and to seek and destroy enemy bases and supply caches. During this mission Thua Thien province became 'Screaming Eagle' country: 3,299 enemy were killed, 853 prisoners were captured and 3,702 weapons were taken. The 101st discovered and removed enough rice to feed 10 enemy battalions for a year.

On July 1, 1968, during the 'Nevada Eagle' operation, the division's name was changed to the 101st Air Cavalry Division. This name

lasted until August 29, 1969 when the 'Screaming Eagles' became the 101st Airborne Division (Airmobile), creating the Army's second airmobile division (the 1st Cavalry Division was the first) and symbolizing the transition from parachutes to helicopters.

On July 1, 1968 at Camp Eagle in Vietnam, the 160th Aviation Group was constituted. It was redesignated the 101st Aviation Group in 1969 and this group began delivering the 'Screaming Eagles' to the battlefield by helicopter, using UH-1H Hueys and CH-47 Chinooks, plus AH-1 Cobras and scout helicopters from 2nd Squadron, 17th Cavalry Regiment.

'Apache Snow' and 'Hamburger Hill'

One of the most important Viet Cong and NVA supply routes and staging areas was the A Shau valley, which ran along the western edge of Thua Thien province. Prior to 'Nevada Eagle', the 1st Brigade undertook a 17-day operation called 'Somerset Plain'. On completion of 'Nevada Eagle', the 101st again attacked the A Shau valley in a series of operations: 'Massachusetts Striker', 'Apache Snow' and 'Montgomery Rendezvous'.

During 'Apache Snow', in May and June 1969, the 3rd Battalion of the 187th Infantry assaulted Dong Ap Bia mountain (Hill 937; Hamburger Hill) in one of the most famous and controversial battles of the war. The

Right
Members of the 2–327th Infantry enter the A Shau Valley during the first operation in the communist haven in almost two years. The 'Screaming Eagles' discovered an enemy base-camp of several hundred bunkers which was abandoned only hours before their arrival.

mountain was captured by a classic infantry assault on May 20, 1969. These operations decimated the enemy forces and forced the NVA to place more reliance upon supply bases in neighbouring Laos.

During 1969 through 1970 the division became involved in the United States' civil operations in the pacification program. Operation 'Randolph Glen' required the 101st to provide technical assistance to government officials of Thua Thien province. While assisting in the development and pacification of the province, elements of the 101st worked with the Army of the Republic of Vietnam (ARVN). Operations 'Texas Star' and 'Jefferson Glen' followed: using a network of fire-support bases and aggressive patrolling, the 'Screaming Eagles' prevented enemy thrusts into Thua Thien province. For its involvement in numerous civil affairs programs, the

101st received the Vietnamese Civic Action Medal on May 23, 1970.

'Lam Son 719'

In April through June 1970 the 101st participated in a limited incursion into Cambodia. The most important test for the airmobile concept came in February 1971 during operation 'Lam Son 719'. During this operation the 101st Aviation Group supported Vietnamese forces in an attack across the Laotian border designed to cut enemy infiltration routes and to destroy North Vietnamese staging areas in Laos. The operation began on February 8, when the 101st and other aviation units airlifted ARVN troops into Laos. During 'Lam Son 719' the U.S. helicopter units found that, with the onset of the rainy season, early morning fog and low cloud restricted their flight paths through the mountains. The airmobile operation involved not only troop-carrying UH-1H/UH-1C helicopters but included the full airmobile concept, including the use of air cavalry troops (2/17th Cav) supported by AH-1G Cobras providing escort and security of landing zones

as well as eliminating enemy AA guns. CH-47 Chinook and CH-53s were also used for heavy-lift tasks.

When 'Lam Son 719' ended on April 9, 1971 the combined air and ground operations conducted along the Laotian/South Vietnamese border had resulted in 13,914 enemy killed, 106 tanks destroyed and more than 5,500 weapons destroyed or captured. The NVA employed a greater degree of fire support during this operation than at any other time in the war. Despite the NVA's increased use of anti-aircraft weapons, artillery and armor, less than one allied aircraft for every 1,000 sorties was lost.

'Lam Son 720' soon followed. ARVN soldiers of the 1st Infantry Division, supported by the 101st, invaded the A Shau valley and cut enemy supply routes. For its action from March to October 1971, the 101st received the Vietnamese Cross of Gallantry with Palm.

In late 1971 and early 1972 the 101st withdrew and redeployed to the United States. They were the last U.S. Army division to leave the combat zone in Vietnam. Vice President Spiro T. Agnew and Army Chief of

Above
SP4 Leland W. Books, A/2–502 Infantry gives a wounded buddy water from his canteen as they wait for a MEDEVAC helicopter during 'Operation Nevada Eagle'.

Staff General William C. Westmoreland welcomed the 101st during official homecoming ceremonies on April 6, 1972 at Fort Campbell, Kentucky.

After Vietnam, it was not until June 1973 that the division, under the 'Unit of Choice' recruiting program, reached combat-ready status again. In 1974 the 101st had a significant identity change when, on February 1, the 3rd Brigade announced the termination of its parachute status and Major General Sidney B. Berry, the commanding general, authorized the wearing of an airmobile badge.

Air Assault

On 4th October 1974 the airmobile designation was dropped and the division added the parenthetical Air Assault designation to its name. The division formed its Air Assault School at Fort Campbell and graduated its first students in March 1974. Graduates received a newly designed air-assault badge, which officially became an army qualifications skill badge on January 20, 1978, retroactive to April 1974 for any soldier in an air-assault unit who had demonstrated the necessary professional knowledge and skill.

Over the next few years the 101st continually tested the air-assault concept in exercises all over the globe. As the only air-assault division in the world, the 101st devised and tested new combined-arms tactics and doctrines. In June 1979 the division received the first of its new UH-60A Black Hawk helicopters and integrated them into the air-assault concept.

Fulfilling its readiness role under the 'one army' concept, the division played a vital part in helping the United States meet her commitment in the Middle East. Between November 7 and 25, 1980 elements of the division participated in the rapid-deployment joint task force exercise 'Bright Star' near Cairo, Egypt. The contingent consisted of a battalion combat team of 900 men from 1st Battalion of the 501st Infantry, along with supporting units. The exercise gave the division experience in overseas movement, desert warfare, and coordination with other branches of the United States' armed forces and with foreign allies. Since then, several other exercises involving the Rapid Deployment Force have been carried out. The

division's battalions annually train in the Panama jungle, desert-train in California and winter-train in Alaska. In their rapid-deployment role the division must have a battalion-size unit ready to deploy within 12 hours, and a brigade-size force ready within 18 hours, and capable of fighting anywhere in the world.

In late March 1982, the XVII Airborne Corps designated the 1st Battalion of the 502nd Infantry as the replacement unit to be sent to the Sinai peninsula in Egypt for a six-month tour of duty with the U.N. Multinational Force and Observers (MFO) operation. Supporting the American commitment to the peacekeeping force established under the terms of the 1979 Egypt–Israeli peace treaty, the 'Screaming Eagles' and the 82nd Airborne Division from Fort Bragg alternated six-month tours of duty.

In 1983 the division was reorganized under a new regimental system. The 327th, the 502nd and the 187th Regiments became the brigades for the division. The 327th and 502nd had been two of the division's original units in 1942. The 187th has the distinction of being the only airborne unit to see active service in World War II, Korea and Vietnam. While implementing the new regimental system throughout 1984, the division participated in 15 major exercises in the United States, West Germany, Honduras and Egypt, fulfilling its assigned mission to deploy rapidly worldwide using the unique capabilities of the air-assault division.

Tragedy struck the 101st on December 12, 1985, when 248 members of the 3rd Battalion of the 502nd Infantry perished in an airline crash near Gander, Newfoundland. The battalion was returning from a routine tour of duty as part of the MFO contingent in Sinai.

The air-assault concept continues to provide strategic mobility with the extremely high degree of tactical mobility needed on today's and tomorrow's battlefields. In February 1984 the division took delivery of the first of 45 CH-47 'D' model Chinook helicopters, and in December 1988 these were followed by the first of 38 AH-64A Apache attack helicopters. These new helicopters and continually evolving doctrine have significantly improved the division's flexibility and fire-power.

DIVISION FACTS

Note: The campaigns and unit awards listed are for Headquarters and Headquarters Company, 101st Airborne Division (Air Assault). Individual units within the division may have more campaign credits or unit awards. This can be determined by referring to the unit's lineage and honors statement. Each unit has an official lineage and honors statement in its historian's file.

UNIT DAY-15 August

CAMPAIGNS
World War II
Normandy
Rhineland
Ardennes-Alsace
Central Europe

Republic of Vietnam
Counteroffensive, Phase III
Tet Counteroffensive
Counteroffensive, Phase IV
Counteroffensive, Phase V
Counteroffensive, Phase VI
Tet 1969, Counteroffensive
Summer–Fall 1969
Winter–Spring 1970
Counteroffensive, Phase VII
Sanctuary Counteroffensive
Consolidation I
Consolidation II

DECORATIONS
World War II
Presidential Unit Citation (Army), streamer embroidered NORMANDY
Presidential Unit Citation (Army), streamer embroidered BASTOGNE
French Croix-de-Guerre with Palm, streamer embroidered NORMANDY
Belgian Croix-de-Guerre with Palm, streamer embroidered BASTOGNE
Belgian Fourragère
Netherlands Orange Lanyard

Republic of Vietnam
Republic of Vietnam Civil Action Medal, First Class, streamer embroidered VIETNAM 1968–1970 (HHC)
Republic of Vietnam Cross of Gallantry with Palm, streamer embroidered VIETNAM 1968–1969 (HHC)
Republic of Vietnam Cross of Gallantry with Palm, streamer embroidered VIETNAM 1971 (101st Airborne Division)

DIVISION COMMANDERS

MG William C. Lee	Aug 42–Feb 44
†*MG Maxwell D. Taylor	Mar 44–Aug 45
BG William M. Gillmore	Aug–Sep 45
BG Gerald St. Clair Mickle	Sep–Oct 45
BG Stuart Cutler	Oct–Nov 45
MG William R. Schmidt	Jul 48–May 49
MG Cornelius E. Ryan	Aug 50–May 51
MG Ray E. Porter	May 51–May 53
MG Paul DeWitt Adams	May–Dec 53
MG Riley F. Ennis	May 54–Oct 55
MG F.S. Bowen	Oct 55–Mar 56
MG Thomas L. Sherburne, Jr.	May 56–Mar 58
†MG William C. Westmoreland	Apr 58–Jun 60
MG Ben Harrell	Jun 60–Jul 61
MG Charles W.G. Rich	Jul 61–Feb 63
MG Harry W. Critz	Feb 63–Mar 64
MG Beverley E. Powell	Mar 64–Mar 66
MG Ben Sternberg	Mar 66–Jul 67
*MG Olinto M. Barsanti	Jul 67–Jul 68
MG Melvin Zais	Jul 68–May 69
*MG John M. Wright	May 69–May 70
*MG John J. Hennessey	May 70–Feb 71
*MG Thomas M. Tarpley	Feb 71–Apr 72
MG John W. Cushman	Apr 72–Aug 73
MG Sidney B. Berry	Aug 73–Jul 74
MG John W. McEnery	Aug 74–Feb 76
†MG John A. Wickham, Jr.	Mar 76–Mar 78
MG John N. Brandenburg	Mar 78–Jun 80
MG Jack V. Mackmull	Jun 80–Aug 81
MG Charles W. Bagnal	Aug 81–Aug 83
MG James E. Thompson	Aug 83–Jun 85
MG Burton D. Patrick	Jun 85–May 87
MG T.G. Allen	May 87–Aug 1989
MG J.H. Binford-Peay III	Aug 89–Present

*Combat commanders
†Later served as army chief of staff

Note: BG Don F. Pratt (Feb 6 to Mar 14, 1944) and BG Anthony C. McAuliffe (Dec 5–26, 1944) are frequently listed as division commanders when actually they were acting division commanders. They, like other acting commanders, do not appear on this list.

INDEX

Page numbers in bold refer to an illustration

ACKNOWLEDGEMENTS

The publishers and the author would like to thank the following for their kind help and assistance:
Major General J.H. Binford-Peay III, Commanding Officer, 101st Airborne Division (Air Assault).
Lieut Col Richard M. Bridges, Media Relations Division, Department of the Army, Washington, D.C.
Major Dan Grigson, Public Affairs Officer, and Bill Harralson, Deputy Public Affairs Officer, 101st Airborne Division (Air Assault) and Fort Campbell.

Special thanks are due to Master Sergeant Steve Sanderson of the Public Affairs Office, 101st Airborne Division (Air Assault) and Fort Campbell for all the invaluable help and assistance.

Our thanks also to Tony Kirves of Southern Exposure, Hopkinsville, Kentucky, for his untiring efforts, and to Rose Tooley.

We would also like to thank the staff of the Don F. Pratt Museum at Fort Campbell for allowing us access to their photographic records. Much of the material used in this book is derived from the division history booklet prepared by Dr Robert F. Schrader, Division/Post Historian.

The photographs of the Ch-47D Chinook on pages 23 and 101 are reproduced by kind courtesy of the Boeing Helicopter Company.

Book design: Hussain R. Mohamed.